POISONOUS SNAKES
IN THE REPUBLIC OF BENIN

DALLYS-TOM MEDALI

POISONOUS SNAKES
IN THE REPUBLIC BENIN

ISBN: 978-1-947838-13-0

###
Solara Editions
New York, Paris, Cotonou
###
Cover Design: Dallys-Tom Medali

###

Poisonous Snakes in Benin

- Atheris chlorechis

- Atractaspis dahomeyensis

- Atractaspis irregularis

- Atractaspis microlepidota

- Bitis arietans (most common in Africa)

- Bitis gabonica (deadliest)

- Bitis nasicornis

- Boiga blandingii

- Causus lichtensteinii

- Causus maculatus

- Dendroaspis jamesoni

- Dendroaspis viridis

- Dispholidus typus

- Echis leucogaster

- Echis ocellatus (most common in Benin)

- Elapsoidea semiannulata

- Naja haje

- Naja katiensis

- Naja melanoleuca (most dangerous)

- Naja nigricollis

- Pseudohaje nigra

- Thelotornis kirtlandii

Atheris chlorechis

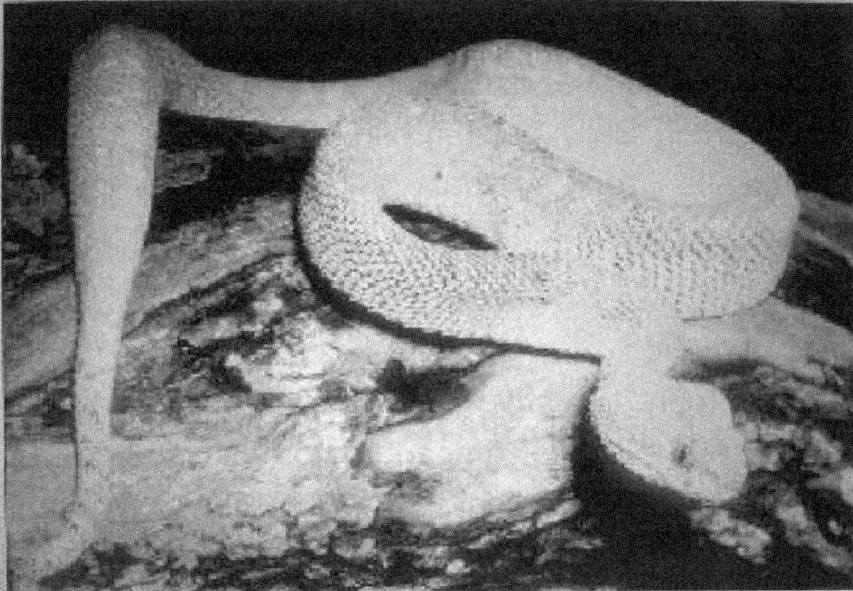

Identification

Family: Viperidae
Scientific Names: Atheris chloroechis, A. squamiger chlorechis, A. polylepis, Echis chloroechis, Toxicoa chloroechis, Vipera chlorechis, V. chloroechis
Common Names: Western bush viper

Description

Medium-sized arboreal adder, adults usually 45-55 cm long (max. 70+ cm), with 25-36 mid-body dorsal rows of keeled scales. Body usually uniform pale-green above, darkening a little on sides and toward tail. Belly paler green. Tail long, strongly prehensile. Young usually with tail tipped with sulphur-yellow.

Habitat

Mainly found in green shrubs and foliage fairly near ground in west African rainforests. Limited to tropical and subtropical western African countries (mainly from Guinea eastward to Ghana).

Activity and Behavior

Strongly arboreal (within 1-2 m of ground), but rarely hunts small rodent prey at ground level. Mainly nocturnal or crepuscular (active at dusk and dawn), but may bask in sun. Ovoviviparous with usually 6-9 young/ litter.

Venom Characteristics

Not well known, but venom likely hemotoxic, although no record of human bites. No known specific antivenom currently produced.

Atractaspis dahomeyensis

Identification

Family: Atractaspididae
Scientific Names:
Common Names: Dahomey burrowing viper, mole viper, Dahomey burrowing asp

Description

Juveniles are very thin, but big adults can be very stout. Average 29-35 middorsal scale rows. Dark brown, grey, pinkish-grey, or black in color, paler below. One albino specimen recorded from Ghana. Also See Atractaspis bibronii.

Habitat

Found in savannahs from southwestern Camaroon west and north through Nigeria, Benin, Togo, Ghana, northwestern Ivory Coast, southwestern Burkina Faso, and south-central Mali. Also recorded from western Mali and northern Guinea, and one record from a forest in Ivory Coast.

Activity and Behavior

Not much known, but probably mainly fossorial, active above ground after rains, and mainly nocturnal. Probably oviparous (with small No. of eggs) and eats available lizards, other snakes, and small mammals.

Venom Characteristics

In a series of envenomations in Nigeria, victims had pain at the bite site, developed local swelling which reached its maximum within 24 hrs., and usually resolved within 5 days. Some victims had swollen, tender lymph nodes and mild fever, but no necrosis was noted.

Atractaspis irregularis

Identification

Family: Atractaspididae
Scientific Names: Atractaspis irregularis angeli, A. i. bipostocularis, A. i. conradsi, A. i. irregularis, A. i. parkeri, A. i. uelensis, A. bipostocularis, A. caudalis, A. conradsi, Elaps irregularis
Common Names: Variable burrowing asp, mole viper

Description

Medium-sized, stout-bodied, burrowing asp, adults avg. 30-50 cm long (max. about 65 cm), with smooth dorsal scales in 23-27 (rarely 21) mid-body rows. Body usually black or blackish-gray, belly often lighter. For more generalized characters of this group, based on a closely-related species, See Atractaspis bibronii.

Habitat

Mainly found in forests, forest edges, high grasslands, and savannaahs (but not arid areas) across most equatorial zone of western and central Africa. For typical local habitats occupied by a closely related species, See Atractaspis bibronii.

Activity and Behavior

Not well known, but mainly nocturnal and fossorial. Routinely burrows in loose, sandy soil or under surface debris. Active on top of ground after rains. Probably oviparous with <10 eggs/ clutch; and eats available lizards, other snakes and other small animals. Known to eat rodents. Also See Atractaspis bibronii.

Venom Characteristics

Not much known, but probably has cardiotoxic factor(s). Envenomation symptoms similar to those for other burrowing asps. At least 2 human fatalities documented due to a bites by this species, but each of those was under unusual circumstances. Also See Atractaspis bibronii.

Atractaspis microlepidota

Identification

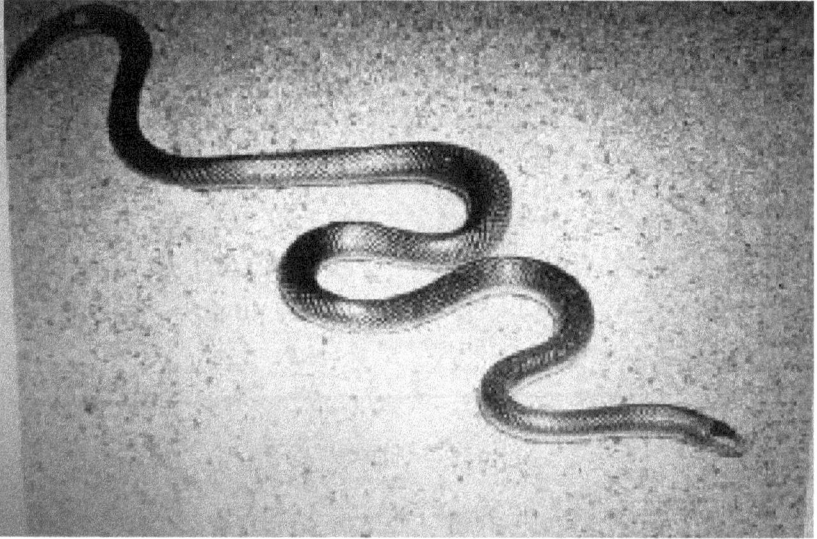

Family: Atractaspididae
Scientific Names: Atractaspis microlepidota andersonii, A. m. magrettii, A. m. microlepidota, A. andersonii, A. magrettii, A. micropholis, A. phillipsi
Common Names: Small-scaled burrowing asp, mole viper, jilbris, "the snake of 7 steps", "father of 10 minutes"

Description

One of biggest burrowing asps, adults avg. 30-80 cm long (max. 1.1 m), big individuals remarkably stout. Dorsal scales smooth and in 25-37 mid-body rows. Body shiny black, purplish-black, deep grey, or very dark brown body (rarely with white tail tip), may be irridescent gray below with very short, broad head.

Habitat

Found mainly in semi-desert and dry savannahs of the Sahel; from Senegal and Mauritania to Chad including Benin, southern and northeastern Sudan, and low elevation regions of Ethiopia, Somalia, and Kenya. Also known from southwestern Arabian penninsula and Sinai.

Activity and Behavior

Nocturnal and fossorial (burrowing), but not well known. Relatively fast moving at night and active on top of ground after rains. Strikes quickly, to one side and backwards, if disturbed, restrained or stepped on. Oviparous with 8 eggs laid by a captured female. Eats available lizards, other snakes, and other small animals.

Venom Characteristics

Not very well known, has cardiotoxic factor(s) and causes symptoms similar to those caused by venom of related species; local pain, swelling, nausea, vomiting, and diarrhoea. Venom glands very long, extend 8-12 cm into the snake's neck, bite reported to usually yield rather low volume of venom. Many serious envenomations of humans; at least 3 human fatalities documented. For a similar species, See Atractaspis bibronii.

Bitis arietans

Identification

Family: Viperidae / Scientific Names: Bitis arietans

The word "arietans" means "striking violently"
Common Names: puff adder, common puff adder,
African puff adder

Description

The average size is about 1m (39.3 inches) in total length (body + tail) and very stout. Large specimens of 190 cm (75 in) total length, weighing over 6.0 kg (13.2 lbs) and with a girth of 40 cm (16 in) have been reported. Males are usually larger than females and have relatively longer tails. The head has a less than triangular shape with a blunt and rounded snout. Still, the head is much wider than the neck. The rostral scale is small. The circumorbital ring consists of 10–16 scales. Mid-body there are 29–41 rows of dorsal scales. These are strongly keeled except for the outermost rows. The ventral scale count is 123–147, the subcaudals 14–38. Females have no more than 24 subcaudals. The anal scale is single.

The color pattern varies geographically. The head has two well-marked dark bands: one on the crown and the other between the eyes. On the sides of the head, there are two oblique dark bands or bars that run from the eye to the supralabials. Below, the head is yellowish white with scattered dark blotches. Iris color ranges from gold to silver-gray. Dorsally, the ground-color varies from straw yellow, to light brown, to orange or reddish brown. This is overlaid with a pattern of

18–22 backwardly-directed, dark brown to black bands that extend down the back and tail. Usually these bands are roughly chevron-shaped, but may be more U-shaped in some areas. They also form 2–6 light and dark cross-bands on the tail. Some populations are heavily flecked with brown and black, often obscuring other coloration, giving the animal a dusty-brown or blackish appearance. The belly is yellow or white, with a few scattered dark spots. Newborn and young have golden head markings with pinkish to reddish ventral plates toward the lateral edges.

This species is probably the most common and widespread snake in Africa. It is found in most of sub-Saharan Africa including in Benin. It also occurs on the Arabian peninsula.

Habitat

It is found in all habitats except true deserts, rain forests, and (tropical) alpine habitats. It is most often associated with rocky grasslands.

Activity and Behavior

Normally a sluggish species, it relies on camouflage for protection. Locomotion is primarily rectilinear, using the broad ventral scales in a caterpillar fashion and aided by its own weight for traction. When agitated, it can resort to a fast serpentine movement. Although mainly terrestrial, these snakes are good swimmers and can also climb with ease; often they are found basking in low bushes. One specimen was found 4.6 m above the ground in a densely branched tree.

If disturbed, they will hiss loudly and continuously, adopting a tightly coiled defensive posture with the fore part of their body held in a taut "S" shape. At the same time, they may attempt to back away from the threat towards cover. They may strike suddenly and fast, to the side as easily as forwards, before returning quickly to the defensive position, ready to strike again. During a strike, the force of the impact is so strong, and the long fangs penetrate so deeply, that prey items are often killed by the physical trauma alone. The fangs apparently can penetrate soft leather.

They can strike to a distance of about one third of their body length, but juveniles will launch their entire bodies forwards in the process. These snakes rarely grip their victims, instead releasing quickly to return to the striking position.

Mostly nocturnal, they rarely forage actively, preferring instead to ambush prey as it happens by. Their prey includes mammals, birds, amphibians, and lizards.

Females produce a pheromone to attract males, which engage in neck-wrestling combat dances. They give birth to large numbers of offspring: litters of over 80 have been reported, while 50–60 is not unusual. Newborns are 12.5–17.5 cm in length. These snakes do well in captivity, but there are reports of gluttony. Kauffeld (1969) mentions that specimens can be maintained for years on only one meal per week, but that when offered all they can eat, the result is often death, or at best wholesale regurgitation. They are bad-tempered snakes and some specimens never settle down in captivity, always hissing and puffing when approached.

Venom Characteristics

This species is responsible for more snakebite fatalities than any other African snake. This is due to a combination of factors, including its wide distribution, common occurrence, large size, potent venom that is produced in large amounts, long fangs, their habit of basking by footpaths and sitting quietly when approached.

The venom has cytotoxic effects and is one of the most toxic of any vipers. Venom yield is typically between 150–350 mg, with a maximum of 750 mg. About 100 mg is thought to be enough to kill a healthy adult human male, with death occurring after 25 hours.

In humans, bites from this species can produce severe local and systemic symptoms and can be divided into two categories: those with little or no surface extravasation, and those with hemorrhages evident as ecchymosis, bleeding and swelling. In both cases there is severe pain and tenderness, but in the latter there is widespread superficial or deep necrosis and compartment syndrome. Serious bites cause limbs to become immovably flexed as a result of significant hemorrhage or coagulation in the affected muscles. Other bite symptoms that may occur in humans include edema, which may become extensive, shock, watery blood oozing from the puncture wounds, nausea and vomiting, subcutaneous bruising, blood blisters that may form rapidly, and a painful swelling of the regional lymph nodes. Swelling usually decreases after a few days, except for the area immediately around the bite site. Hypotension, together with weakness, dizziness and periods of semi- or unconsciousness is also reported.

If not treated carefully, necrosis will spread, causing skin, subcutaneous tissue and muscle to separate from healthy tissue and eventually slough with serous exudate. The slough may be superficial or deep, sometimes down to the bone. Gangrene and secondary infections commonly occurs and can result in loss of digits and limbs.

The fatality rate highly depends on the severity of the bites and some other factors. Deaths can be exceptional and probably occur in less than 15% of all untreated cases (usually in 2–4 days from complications following blood volume deficit and a disseminated intravascular coagulopathy), although some reports show that severe envenomations have a 52% mortality rate. Most fatalities are associated with poor clinical management and neglect.

Bitis gabonica

Identification

Family: Viperidae
Scientific Names: Bitis gabonica gabonica, B. g. rhinoceros, B. rhinoceros, Cerastes nasicornis, Chlotho rhinoceros, Echidna gabonicus, E. rhinoceros, Urobelus gabonicus, Vipera rhinoceros
Common Names: Gaboon viper, Gaboon adder, Gabunviper

Description

Heavy, thick body, adults average 1.2-1.5 m long (max. 2.0 m), and weigh 8.5 kg. Head up to 12.5 cm wide, fangs up to 55 mm long, with 2 horn-like knobs on top of snout. Beautifully marked; with complex pattern of cream, purple, brown, and pink. Head white or cream above, with thin dark line down middle, an obvious dark-brown triangle from each eye down and backward to upper labials. Belly buff-colored with dark grey blotches. Has 28-41 mid-body scale rows, most dorsal scales keeled.

Habitat

Generally found in tropical rain forests and immediate environs. Sometimes persist in deforested areas. Well camouflaged; blends in with leaf litter of forest floor. Widely distributed in central, eastern and southern Africa; with a subspecies noted for its long nasal horn restricted to western Africa.

Activity and Behavior

Nocturnal. May be found basking in patch of sunlight on forest floor, but more likely to be half-buried in leaf litter. Usually slow-moving and does not flee when approached. Makes very loud hissing noise when disturbed. Strikes only as last resort or if stepped on.

Venom Characteristics

Longest fangs of any snake species in the world, often 40 mm long (max. 55 mm), which enable it to inject massive amounts of potent cytotoxic venom deep into a victim. Venom also contains cardiotoxins that possess neurotoxic properties which may be more dangerous than the cytotoxins.

Bitis nasicornis

Identification

Family: Viperidae

Scientific Names: Cerastes nasicornis, Clotho nasicornis, Coluber nasicornis, Echidna nasicornis, Vipera hexacera, V. nasicornis
Common Names: Rhinoceros viper, River Jack, Nashomviper

Description

Large, stout, with a narrow flat triangular head with small keeled scales. Adults average 60-90 cm long (max. 150 cm), 31-43 mid-body scale rows.

Background color varies; patterned with various geometric shapes in pale blue, red, lemon yellow, green, purple, white, and jet black. Head blue or green with distinctive black arrow mark, belly dirty-white to dull green with lots of black and grey blotches.

Habitat

Found mainly in rain forests, swamps, marshes, and floodplains; river, stream, and lake shores. Seldom goes into woodlands. Well camouflaged among fallen leaves of forest floor. Sometimes tolerated by Kenyan villagers as it resides in roofs of their huts.

Activity and Behavior

Mainly nocturnal, partially aquatic, climbs well; often basks in shrubs and trees. Usually lethargic and slow to strike even in self-defense. Makes loud hissing noise if provoked, but usually is reluctant to strike.

Venom Characteristics

Few bites of humans recorded; however, venom highly cytotoxic. May cause massive swelling and tissue necrosis. Tissue necrosis resulting in amputation has been reported.

Boiga blandingii

Identification

Family: Colubridae
Scientific Names: Dipsas blandingii, D. fasciatus, D. globiceps, Disas valida, Toxicodryas blandingii
Common Names: Blanding's tree snake, Blanding's cat snake, Blanding's broad-headed snake

Description

Large, stocky, rear-fanged tree snake with thin neck, short, broad, flattened head and prominent yellowish to brown eyes set well forward, with vertical pupils. Adults usually 1.4-2.0 m long (max. 2.8 m). Two basic color patterns: Glossy black above - yellow below; or brown, grey or yellow-brown above - yellow-brown below. Large, velvety dorsal scales in 21-25 rows at mid-body. Usually males are black, females and juveniles brownish, some with irregular blackish bars.

Habitat

Primarily found in forested areas, also found in thick woodland/forest-savanna, wooded valleys in grassland, and along gallery forest in savanna areas. Has been reported from a broad band of central Africa, from Guinea in the west to western Kenya and northern Angola. Sometimes enters houses to catch roosting bats.

Activity and Behavior

Nocturnal; rests in leaf clumps, tree hollows, etc., during the day. Mainly arboreal, can climb to 30 m in large trees, but will descend to the ground to cross open spaces and roads. When threatened, it may inflate its body, flatten its head, raise its body in "C-shaped" coils and make bluffing strikes which are seldom on target. Lays 7-14 eggs (20 x 40 mm)/ clutch, eats birds, arboreal lizards, bats and rodents.

Venom Characteristics

Apparently neurotoxic (causing myoneural dysfunction), but not well characterized; No specific antivenom is currently produced and no commercial antivenom is known to be effective. This species will often bite repeatedly, in rapid succession, when threatened. Has caused locally painful bites, but no documented fatalities of humans.

Causus lichtensteinii

Identification

Family: Viperidae
Scientific Names: Aspidelaps lichtensteinii, Dinodipsas angulifera, Heterodon lichtensteinii
Common Names: Forest night adder, Lichtenstein's night adder

Description

Small, medium-built night adder, adults usually 30-55 cm long (max. 70 cm). Body usually olive-green, sometimes with indistinct dark blotches, bars or chevron markings along its back, distinct white, forward- pointed V-shaped mark atop its neck; short, blunt tail. Head pointed and tip up-turned. Dorsal scales velvety, slightly-keeled, in 15 mid-body rows. Belly yellowish, cream or pearly. Juveniles often darker above and below.

Habitat

Found mainly in forests and woodlands of southeastern Africa, from Sierra Leon east to Ghana, in Nigeria east to western Kenya, south to northern Angola, with isolated records from Sudan, Zaire, Zambia.

Activity and Behavior

Mainly terrestrial but climbs into low bushes, mainly nocturnal but often active by day and at twilight, oviparous (4-8 eggs/ clutch). Preys mainly on frogs and toads.

Venom Characteristics

Not much known, but probably mainly hemotoxic. Not considered lethal to man. No known antivenom currently produced.

Causus maculatus

Identification

Family: Viperidae
Scientific Names: Causus rhombeatus (in part), Distichurus maculatus Common Names: Spotted night adder, West African night adder

Description

Small, stout adder, with short head, adults usually about 50 cm long; body usually grayish, brownish, or olive green with darkish rhomboidal marks along dorsum. Dorsal scales velvety, weakly-keeled, in 17-22 mid-body rows, sometimes with a dark vertebral line. Top of head and neck have a large, dark-edged forward- pointing V-shaped mark. Rarely with no dorsal markings in light colored, sandy areas. Snout pointed and up-turned. Belly white, cream or pinkish-grey, may have faint thin darker cross-bars.

Habitat

Found in very wide variety of habitats in a band across western and central Africa; from forest to savanna to semi-desert. Present from senegal east to central Chad, southeast to Zaire, northeast into SE Sudan, and the low country and river gorges of SW Ethiopia, then southwest to northern Angola.

Activity and Behavior

Mainly nocturnal but sometimes active in day or at dusk, and mainly terrestrial but may climb low bushes, sometimes basks in sun. When threatened, inflates body and hisses loudly, not agressive but will bite quickly if further molested. Oviparous with 6-20 eggs/ clutch reported. Prey mainly on available frogs, lizards, and sometimes small mammals or birds.

Venom Characteristics

Not well known. Mainly hemotoxic, with possible cytotoxic factors. Bites generally cause immediate local pain, at least limited local swelling, sometimes fever, and painful regional lymphadenopathy. Second most common cause of snake-bite mortality in Senegal. No known antivenom currently produced.

Dendroaspis jamesoni

Identification

Family: Elapidae
Scientific Names: Dendraspis angusticeps, D. jamesoni, D. jamesonii, D. neglectus, D. welwitschii, Dendroaspis jamesoni jamesoni, D. j. kaimosae, Dinophis fasciolatus, Elaps jamesoni
Common Names: Jameson's mamba, Jameson-Mamba

Description

Large, slender, with narrow head, smooth, narrow scales, adults usually 1.5-2.2 m long (max. 2.5 m); usually dull-green above, pale-green below; scales narrowly edged with black; with 15-17 mid-body dorsal scale rows. Overall color becomes darker toward tail. Long thin tail all black (or with "netlike" yellow and black pattern in some populations). Eyes rather small (vs. large eyes in boomslangs).

Habitat

Tropical rain forest regions, woodlands, and sometimes isolated patches of thick vegetation with one or more trees. Found throughout equatorial tropical forest belt of central and western Africa, from Kenya to Ghana and south to Angola and Burundi.

Activity and Behavior

Arboreal and mainly diurnal, very active and agile, but sometimes descend to the ground. If cornered, it spreads a hood or inflates its throat. Seldom aggressive, but will defend itself if cornered or molested. Oviparous (clutch size not reported) and mainly eats available rodents and birds.

Venom Characteristics

Not well studied. Mainly contains very potent neurotoxins, may also contain some hemotoxic or myotoxic factors. This species is common throughout its range, but bites of humans are rare. Human fatalities have been reported, and seriously envenomated humans may need ventilation support in addition to antivenom therapy.

Dendroaspis viridis

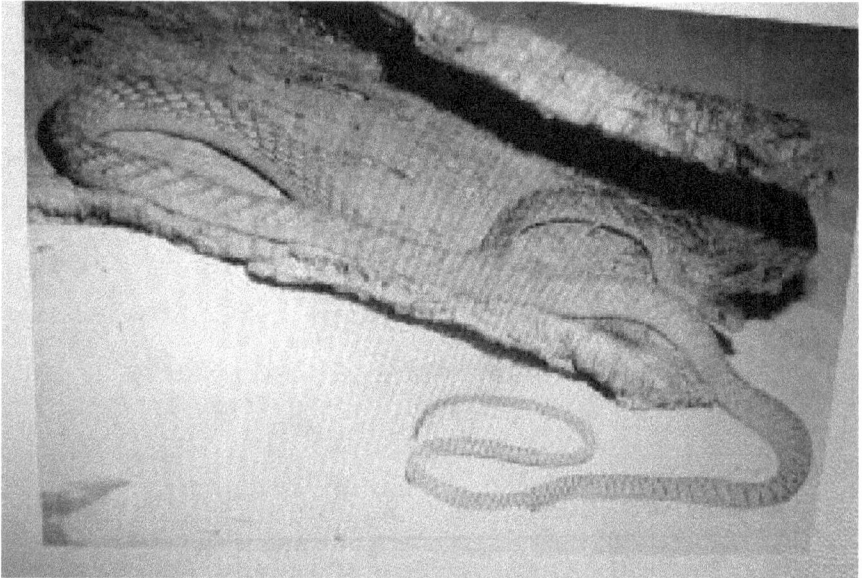

Identification

Family: Elapidae
Scientific Names: Leptophis viridis
Common Names: West African green mamba,
Western green mamba, Grune Mamba

Description

Long, thin, quick-moving alert, green and black
tree snake with narrow head. Adults usually
1.4-2.1 m long (max. 2.3+ m). Usually medium-

green to yellowish-green; scales usually edged with black (especially on head). Smooth dorsal scales relatively very large, in 13 mid-body rows, and long thin tail with yellow scales edged with black. Fixed upper front fangs. Belly pale green.

Habitat

Found mainly in coastal rain forests and, sometimes, isolated patches of thick vegetation with 1 or more trees. Limited to sub-Saharan western Africa, from Nigeria westward to Guinea.

Activity and Behavior

Mainly diurnal and mainly arboreal, but quite often descends to ground if disturbed. Reportedly fairly common throughout its range, but shy and seldom seen. If cornered, may (only very rarely) spread a small hood or inflate its throat. Oviparous (clutch size unknown) and eats mainly available small mammals (e.g., squirrels), birds, and bats.

Venom Characteristics

Venom primarily neurotoxic, but not much known. Potentially dangerous, but bites of humans rare. A few reported envenomations and human deaths due to bites by this species had symptoms very similar to those caused by Black Mamba venom.

Dispholidus typus

Identification

Family: Colubridae
Scientific Names: Bucephalus capensis, B. typus,
Dispholidus typus kivuenis, D. t. punctatus, D. t.
typus Common Names: Boomslang, Grune
Boomslang

Description

Large, rather slender, rear-fanged tree-snake,
adults usually 1.2-1.5 m long (max. 2+ m). May be

black to drab olive-brown, to almost all green; no blotches or distinct spots, juveniles change color (becoming darker and duller) as they become adults. Sexes often different colored. Short stubby head and enormous emerald-green eyes. Scales strongly keeled and overlapping, look like they are in 17-21 diagonal (angled) mid-body dorsal rows.

Habitat

Most common in most kinds of wooded habitats; dry woodlands, thorn scrub, savannas, and swamps bordering or close to streams, rivers, and lakes. Found throughout most of sub-Saharan Africa except continuous rain forests of the Congo basin or true deserts. Reported from

Activity and Behavior

Mainly diurnal, strongly arboreal, spends most of time in trees and shrubs. Notably nonaggressive and shy; quickly retreats if surprised. If cornered, inflates neck to more than twice usual size showing bright yellow or orangish skin beneath. Oviparous, usually lay up to 25 eggs in moist rotting logs on the ground. Prey mainly on tree lizards, birds and eggs, and sometimes arboreal rodents and bats. Do not attempt to constrict prey.

Venom Characteristics

Very potently hemotoxic; can cause severe bleeding internally, within critical organs, and from mucous membranes. Human deaths reported in as short as 3-5 days.

Echis leucogaster

Identification

Family: Viperidae
Scientific Names: Echis arenicola, E. a. leucogaster, Echis carinatus leucogaster, Echis jogeri Common Names: White-bellied carpet viper, Roman's saw-scaled viper

Description

Small, fairly stout, sand viper, adults usually 30-70 cm long (max. 87 cm); color variable, usually brown, gray, or reddish; may have a dorsal series of oblique pale crossbars, interspersed with dark spaces, keeled scales, moveable front fangs, 27-33 mid-body dorsal scale rows. Usually has row of triangular or circular markings along flanks. Belly pale cream, white, or ivory with no markings.

Habitat

Found mainly in arid savanna, semi-desert, and well-vegetated wadis. Not in true desert, but occurs on desert's edge, oases, and elevated vegetated areas within deserts. Mainly limited to arid areas of western Africa.

Activity and Behavior

Mainly nocturnal and terrestrial, but climbs into low bushes to avoid hot or wet surfaces. Can move quickly; most active during first few hours of darkness. Hides in holes, under logs, rocks, and brush piles during daytime. When disturbed, forms C-shaped coils and rubs scales together vigorously, making a loud rustling sound. Mainly eats available lizards and small mammals, but also scorpions and centipedes. Oviparous, clutch size not reported.

Venom Characteristics

Not well known, but probably potent and mainly hemotoxic. Symptomatology likely similar to that of other African carpet vipers including local swelling, incoagulable blood, systemic bleeding, and possibly death.

Echis ocellatus

Identification

Family: Viperidae
Scientific Names: Echis carinatus ocellatus, E. c.
pyramidum Common Names: West African carpet
viper

Description

Small, stout-bodied carpet viper, adults usually
30-50 cm long (max. 65 cm). Body usually brown
or gray or shades in between, with heavily-keeled

scales in 27-34 mid-body dorsal rows. Usually one of 2 different conspicuous dorsal patterns: a series of dark irregular crossbars on lighter background or a series of pale saddles with darker interspaces, belly lighter.

Habitat

Mainly found in Savanna, well-wooded areas, and edges of forests. Limited to western Africa.

Activity and Behavior

Mainly terrestrial, occasionally climbs into low bushes to avoid hot or wet surfaces. Moves rather quickly. Mainly nocturnal; most active during first few hours of darkness. Hides in holes, under logs, rocks, and brush piles during daytime. Not aggressive unless disturbed. Oviparous with usually 6-20 eggs/ clutch. Eats varied prey, including available small mammals, birds, arthropods, lizards, amphibians, and other snakes.

Venom Characteristics

Important cause of snakebite accidents and fatalities almost everywhere it is found; venom highly toxic to man. Venom primarily hemotoxic; internal and external hemorrhages common.

Envenomation usually causes pain and swelling at bite site.

Elapsoidea semiannulata

Identification

Family: Elapidae

Scientific Names: Elapechis boulengeri, E. guentheri, E. sundevallii, Elapsoidea boulengeri, E. decosteri moebiusi, E. d. huilensis, E. guntherii, E. moebiusi, E. semiannulata boulengeri, E. s. moebiusi, E. s. semiannulata, E. sundevallii guentheri, E. s. moebiusi, E. s. semiannulata

Common Names: Half-banded (Africa) garter snake.

Description

Small, moderately stout, glossy, dark snake; adults usually 30-50 cm long (max. 70 cm); body black, short tail, fixed front fangs, smooth-scaled, 13 longitudinal mid-body dorsal scale rows. Young individuals have

8-24 distinct narrow white or yellow cross-bands which fade with age, at about 20 cm long, bands become pale grey and fade, very dark adults may be hard to ID.

Habitat

Found in a wide range of woodlands, savannas and forest clearing edges. Two distinctly separated populations; one from the western-most African coast eastward through northwestern Uganda; the other from the western coast of Angola eastward to the eastern coasts of Tanzania, Zimbabwe and South Africa.

Activity and Behavior

Terrestrial, burrowing, mainly nocturnal, more active just after a rain. Hides in holes, underground cover or under logs in daytime. Inoffensive, can be handled, but may flatten and inflate body if molested, and may even bite if restrained too much. May lift front half of body and jerk body sideways. Eats mainly other snakes, lizards, frogs, and occasionally rodents.

Venom Characteristics

Not much known, probably neurotoxic, but few reported bites of humans, and none of those reported to result in serious bite effects or envenomations of humans, so far.

Naja haje

Identification

Family: Elapidae
Scientific Names: Coluber candidissimus, C. haje,
Cerastes candidus, Naja haje anchietae, N. h.
arabica, N. j. haje, N. h. legionis, N. h. var. viridis,
Vipera haje
Common Names: Egyptian cobra, African banded

cobra, banded cobra, brown cobra, Cleopatra's asp, Arabian cobra

Description

Big, thick-bodied cobra, with broad head and fairly large eyes, adults usually 1.3-1.8 m (max. 2.5 m); body usually yellow-gray to brown or blue-black, but extremely variable. Belly yellowish with dark blotches. Most specimens have dark brown or black band across throat (ventral).

Habitat

Various habitats: flat land, scrubby bushes, grass clumps, irrigated fields, rocky hillsides, old ruins; may hide in old termite mound or rodent burrow; often near villages. Found at sea level to 1,600 m elevation. Not found in rain forests or extreme desert conditions. Geographically widespread in Africa and southern Arabian peninsula.

Activity and Behavior

Nocturnal; emerges at dusk, often seen basking in sun near a retreat in early morning. Often occupies abandoned rodent burrows or termite mounds. While not overtly aggressive, if molested, it will rear and spread an impressive hood up to 12 cm wide. Can bite, and sometimes spreads hood, without rearing. Preys mainly on small mammals.

Venom Characteristics

Venom mainly neurotoxic, affecting nerves controlling respiratory muscles, and possibly with cardio-toxins. Untreated cases may die of respiratory failure, sometimes within 5 hrs. Large volume of venom available, and with relatively large fangs, it can produce serious envenomation. Many human bites and fatalities annually.

Naja katiensis

Identification

Family: Elapidae
Scientific Names: Naja mozambica katiensis, Naja nigricolis katiensis, Naja trilepis Common Names: Mali cobra, West African (brown) spitting cobra

Description

A small, moderately thick-bodied cobra, adults usually 0.5-0.8 m long (max. about 1 m); body usually reddish-brown, warm brown, or maroon, with orange-brown on flanks, belly light orange-brown, with smooth dorsal scales in 23-27 mid-body rows. A broad dark band on underside of throat may form a ring, but this usually fades in older specimens.

Habitat

Found mainly in savannah and semi-desert, from Senegal and southern Mauritania east to Nigeria and Cameroon.

Activity and Behavior

Mainly terrestrial but climbs into low bushes; Mainly crepuscular, but often basks in sun. Fast-moving and alert. Usually tries to get away if disturbed, but if cornered or molested, raises front of its body and spreads a narrow hood. If further disturbed, it often "spits" (sprays) 2 jets of venom at the intruder's head and eyes. Oviparous (clutch size not reported), preys mainly on amphibians, also other snakes and sometimes rodents.

Venom Characteristics

Mainly neurotoxic venom. One of the most common causes of venomous snake bites in Senegal. Has been reported to have caused human deaths.

Naja melanoleuca

Identification

Family: Elapidae
Scientific Names: Aspidelaps bocagii, Naja annulata (in part), Naja haje var. leucosticta, N. h. var. melanoleuca, Naja melanoleuca aurata, N. m. melanoleuca, N. m. subflava
Common Names: Forest cobra, Black-and-white-lipped cobra, White-lipped cobra, Schwarzweisse Kobra

Description

Large, fairly slender cobra, adults usually 1.5-2.0 m long (max. 2.7 m), with 19 mid-body dorsal scale rows. Background color usually glossy black, dark gray or dark brown above; belly creamy white to yellow, often with darker blotches.

Habitat

Found mainly in tropical rain forest and subtropical forest areas, near water. Widespread along rivers and surface waters in central and western Africa.

Activity and Behavior

Mainly nocturnal and terrestrial (maybe semi-aquatic). Very active, climbs and swims well. May forage (hunt) on overcast days. Equally at home in trees, on ground, or swimming in lakes or rivers. When disturbed, rears to a great height; usually more than two-thirds of body raised off ground.

Venom Characteristics

Bites of humans reported infrequent, venom highly neurotoxic; human fatalities have been reported. Considered by many to be one of the most dangerous (to humans) snakes in West Africa, partly due to its aggressive behavior, rapid movement, rather large size, and potent venom.

Naja nigricollis

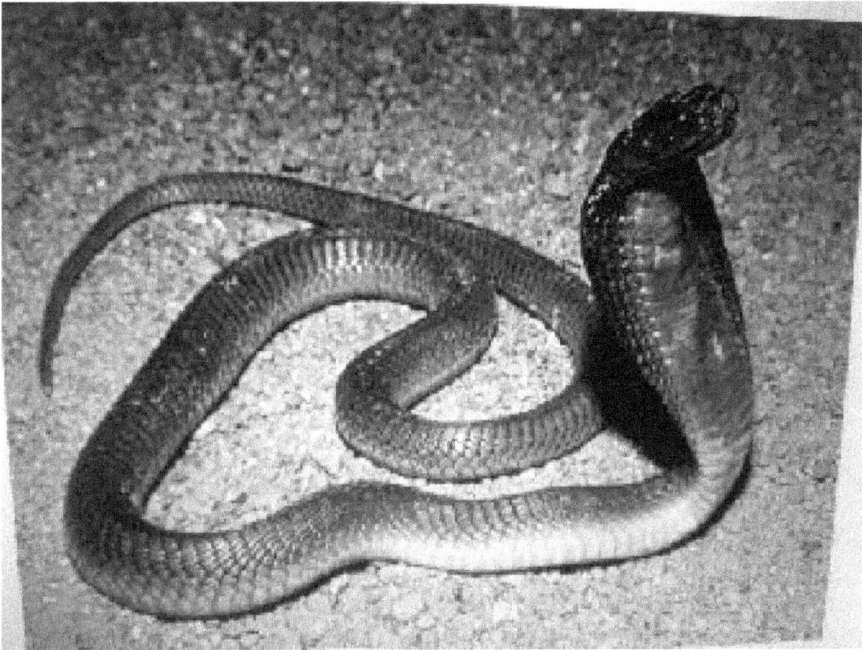

Identification

Family: Elapidae
Scientific Names: Naja mossambica nigricincta,
Naja nigricollis atriceps, N. n. nigricollis, N. n.
nigricincta , N. n. occidentalis, N. n. woodi, N. n.
var. crawshayi, Naja woodi
Common Names: Black-necked spitting cobra,
western barred spitting cobra, black spitting
cobra, Afrikanische Speikobra

Description

Medium to large cobra, adults usually 1.0-1.5 m long (max. 2.8 m). Body color highly variable, ranging from pinkish-tan in some geographical areas to uniformly black in others, most forms have 1 red(ish) and 1 black band across the underside (venter) of their throat. Dorsal scales smooth, with 17-25 rows at mid-body. All-black and red-black specimens have been collected in some areas.

Habitat

Found mainly in moist or dry savanna or sahel, where they shelter in abandoned termite mounds, rodent burrows, or hollow trees. Widespread across many countries in central and southern Africa.

Activity and Behavior

Generally nocturnal (or crepuscular), juveniles often active during day. Mainy terrestrial, but fairly good swimmers and climbers. Oviparous, usually 8-20 eggs/ clutch. Prey on a wide variety of animals, including toads, chickens (often raid chicken runs), other birds and/or eggs, small mammals, and lizards.

Venom Characteristics

Venom primarily cytotoxic, causing serious local tissue damage. Large specimens can "spit" venom as far as 3 m, usually aiming at intruders' eyes (or heads). Venom does not affect unbroken skin, but can cause great pain and possible tissue destruction in the eyes.

Pseudohaje nigra

Identification

Family: Elapidae
Scientific Names: Naia guentheri, Pseudohaje guentheri Common Names: Black tree cobra, hoodless cobra

Description

Big, shiny, thin-bodied tree cobra, adults usually 1.6-2.1 m long (max. 2.2+ m). Body uniformly glossy black or dark brownish-black; ventral surface yellow with no cross-banding; tail long and thin, ending in a spike. Eyes large, prominent, with round pupils; 13 (rarely 15) mid-body dorsal scale rows. Scales on head, chin and throat are yellow, edged with black.

Habitat

Found mainly in forest or thick woodlands, usually near rivers, streams, or in moist riverine forests. Mainly found in countries along the southern coast of West Africa.

Activity and Behavior

Not well known. Rarely encountered. Semi-arboreal. May be both diurnal and nocturnal. Very agile and fast in trees, also very fast on ground. Will pause with head up and alert. Can slightly flatten its neck and threaten if disturbed or cornered. May use tail spike to help defend itself if restrained. Probably preys mainly on small mammals and amphibians. Oviparous, but captives' clutch sizes not reported.

Venom Characteristics

Not much known, but venom is probably very potently neurotoxic, like that of the closely-related species, Gold's tree cobra. Should be considered dangerous, even though no envenomations or fatalities of humans have yet been documented.

Thelotornis kirtlandii

Identification

Family: Colubridae
Scientific Names: Dryiophis kirtlandii, Leptophis kirtlandii, Oxybelis kirtlandii, O. violacea, O. lecomptei, Tragophis rufulus, Thelotornis kirtlandi kirtlandi, Thelotornis kirtlandi oatesi
Common Names: Bird snake, twig snake, forest vine snake, forest twig snake, Lianennatter, Vogelnatter, Graue Baumnatter

Description

Long, very thin tree snake, adults usually 1.0-1.5 m long (max. 1.7 m). Body ashy-gray to pinkish-brown above; uniform or with poorly distinguished blotches and cross-bands anteriorly, 17 mid-body dorsal scale rows, belly paler. Large fixed rear fangs. Long, flat head and eyes with horizontally elongated pupils. Top of head usually solid green, but has turned to solid brown in some captive specimens exposed to strong bright sun.

Habitat

Mainly found in forest and thick woodland, but also in moist savannah and extensive reedbeds. Seems most common around natural glades. Often found in and around farmland, parks, and gardens within forests. Distributed in several equatorial central African countries.

Activity and Behavior

Arboreal; intricate coloration and pattern make it almost invisible when in trees or shrubbery. Usually timid, seldom bitoc unless strongly provoked, then makes spectacular display with greatly (vertically) inflated neck before striking. Eats mainly lizards, birds, and sometimes other snakes. Catches and usually consumes prey while hanging from a bush or tree. Oviparous, with usually 4-12 eggs/ clutch.

Venom Characteristics

Venom mainly hemotoxic; few bites, fewer significant envenomations, and no deaths of humans known to have been caused by this snake.

This book wouldn't have been possible without publicly available information provided by the US ARMY, Wikipedia and Google.

Major Thanks to my mom who involuntarily triggered this book with a random message.

I am dedicating this to my three deceased grandparents: Andre Medali, Andre R. G. Tokpo and Hogbonouto. You guys are no longer in this world but you are forever in our hearts.

OTHER BOOKS BY DALLYS-TOM MEDALI

- 1000 African Heroes (English)
- 30 Years of Painting and Drawing (English)
- Coming Back (English)
- Belles Poésies de Coeur and de Corps (French)
- Essais sur le Bénin (French)
- Héros Africains, Cahier de Recherches (French)
- L'Evangile Pratique (French)
- Le Manuel du Milliardaire (French)
- Légendes Inédites d'Afrique (French)
- Perles and Pensées (French)

http://www.dallystom.com

http://www.heroafricain.com

http://www.milliardaire.org

http://www.benindufutur.org

http://www.briquemagique.com

ISBN: 978-1-947838-13-0

www.ingramcontent.com/pod-product-compliance
Lightning Source LLC
Chambersburg PA
CBHW031524270326
41930CB00006B/515